Technology and Inventions

Get the inside story on gadgets and systems past and present

ENCYCLOPÆDIA

Britannica®

CHICAGO   LONDON   NEW DELHI   PARIS   SEOUL   SYDNEY   TAIPEI   TOKYO

PROJECT TEAM

Judith West, *Editorial Project Manager*
Christopher Eaton, *Editor and Educational Consultant*
Indu Ramchandani, *Project Editor (Encyclopædia Britannica India)*
Bhavana Nair, *Managing Editor (India)*
Rashi Jain, *Senior Editor (India)*
Kathryn Harper, *U.K. Editorial Consultant*
Colin Murphy, *Editor*
Locke Petersheim, *Editor*
Nancy Donohue Canfield, *Creative Director*
Megan Newton-Abrams, *Designer*
Amy Ning, *Illustrator*
Joseph Taylor, *Illustrator*
Karen Koblik, *Senior Photo Editor*
Paul Cranmer, *Retrieval Specialist and Indexer*
Barbara Whitney, *Copy Supervisor*
Laura R. Gabler, *Copy Editor*
Dennis Skord, *Copy Editor*
Marilyn L. Barton, *Senior Production Coordinator*

ENCYCLOPÆDIA BRITANNICA
PROJECT SUPPORT TEAM

EDITORIAL

Theodore Pappas, *Executive Editor*
Lisa Braucher, *Data Editor*
Robert Curley, *Senior Editor, Sciences*
Brian Duignan, *Senior Editor, Philosophy, Law*
Laura J. Kozitka, *Senior Editor, Art, World Culture*
Kathleen Kuiper, *Senior Editor, Music, Literature, World Culture*
Kenneth Pletcher, *Senior Editor, Geography*
Jeffrey Wallenfeldt, *Senior Editor, Geography, Social Sciences*
Anita Wolff, *Senior Editor, General Studies*
Charles Cegielski, *Associate Editor, Astronomy*
Mark Domke, *Associate Editor, Biology*
Michael Frassetto, *Associate Editor, Religion*
James Hennelly, *Associate Editor, Film, Sports*
William L. Hosch, *Associate Editor, Math, Technology*
Michael R. Hynes, *Associate Editor, Geography*
Michael I. Levy, *Associate Editor, Politics, Geography*
Tom Michael, *Associate Editor, Geography*
Sarah Forbes Orwig, *Associate Editor, Social Sciences*
Christine Sullivan, *Associate Editor, Sports, Pastimes*
Erin M. Loos, *Associate Editor, Human Biology*
Anne Eilis Healey, *Assistant Editor, Art, World Culture*

DESIGN

Steven N. Kapusta, *Designer*
Cate Nichols, *Designer*

ART

Kathy Nakamura, *Manager*
Kristine A. Strom, *Media Editor*

ILLUSTRATION

David Alexovich, *Manager*
Jerry A. Kraus, *Illustrator*

MEDIA ASSET MANAGEMENT

Jeannine Deubel, *Manager*
Kimberly L. Cleary, *Supervisor, Illustration Control*
Kurt Heintz, *Media Production Technician*
Quanah Humphreys, *Media Production Technician*

CARTOGRAPHY

Paul Breding, *Cartographer*

COPY

Sylvia Wallace, *Director*
Larry Kowalski, *Copy Editor*
Carol Gaines, *Typesetter*

INFORMATION MANAGEMENT/INDEXING

Carmen-Maria Hetrea, *Director*

EDITORIAL LIBRARY

Henry Bolzon, *Head Librarian*
Lars Mahinske, *Geography Curator*
Angela Brown, *Library Assistant*

EDITORIAL TECHNOLOGIES

Steven Bosco, *Director*
Gavin Chiu, *Software Engineer*
Bruce Walters, *Technical Support Coordinator*
Mark Wiechec, *Senior Systems Engineer*

COMPOSITION TECHNOLOGY

Mel Stagner, *Director*

MANUFACTURING

Dennis Flaherty, *Director*

INTERNATIONAL BUSINESS

Leah Mansoor, *Vice President, International Operations*
Isabella Saccà, *Director, International Business Development*

MARKETING

Patti Ginnis, *Senior Vice President, Sales and Marketing*
Jason Nitschke, *National Sales Manager, Retail Advertising and Syndication*
Michael Ross, *Consultant*

ENCYCLOPÆDIA BRITANNICA, INC.

Jacob E. Safra,
Chairman of the Board

Ilan Yeshua,
Chief Executive Officer

Jorge Cauz,
President

Dale H. Hoiberg,
Senior Vice President and Editor

Marsha Mackenzie,
Managing Editor and Director of Production

Technology and Inventions

INTRODUCTION

How can you draw with light?

What was Gutenberg's gift? Where does medicine come from?

Can eyes ever hear?

In *Technology and Inventions,* you'll discover answers to these questions and many more. Through pictures, articles, and fun facts, you'll learn about the great inventors and inventions that have changed our lives.

To help you on your journey, we've provided the following signposts in *Technology and Inventions*:

■ **Subject Tabs**—The coloured box in the upper corner of each right-hand page will quickly tell you the article subject.

■ **Search Lights**—Try these mini-quizzes before and after you read the article and see how much - *and how quickly* - you can learn. You can even make this a game with a reading partner. (Answers are upside down at the bottom of one of the pages.)

■ **Did You Know?**—Check out these fun facts about the article subject. With these surprising 'factoids', you can entertain your friends, impress your teachers, and amaze your parents.

■ **Picture Captions**—Read the captions that go with the photos. They provide useful information about the article subject.

■ **Vocabulary**—New or difficult words are in **bold type**. You'll find them explained in the Glossary at the end of the book.

■ **Learn More!**—Follow these pointers to related articles in the book. These articles are listed in the Table of Contents and appear on the Subject Tabs.

Britannica
LEARNING LIBRARY

Have a great trip!

**Hot-air balloons fill the skies at the
Albuquerque International Balloon Fiesta
in New Mexico in 1989.**
© Joseph Sohm—Chromosohm Inc./Corbis

Technology and Inventions

TABLE OF CONTENTS

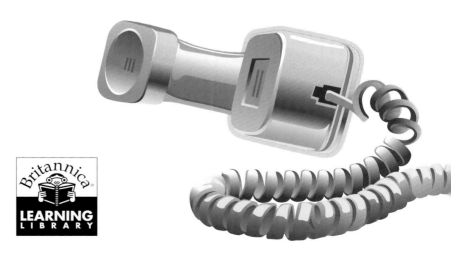

Before There Were Automobiles

Long ago, most people had to walk wherever they wanted to go on land. Later, when large animals began to be **domesticated,** some people rode on camels, horses, donkeys, oxen, and even elephants.

Then came the discovery of wheels. The people of Mesopotamia (now in Iraq) built wheeled carts nearly 5,000 years ago. But so far the earliest cart that has actually been found is one made later than those in Mesopotamia, by people in ancient Rome. It was simply a flat board. At first, people pulled carts themselves. Later, they trained animals to do this.

As people used more and more carts, they had to make roads on which the carts could travel easily. In Europe and North America, carts developed into great covered wagons and then into stagecoaches. Pulled by four or six fast horses, stagecoaches first bounced and rolled along the roads in the mid-1600s. They became an important method of public transport during the 19th century.

It wasn't until the steam engine was invented that a better means of transportation was developed. This was the railway train. Steam **locomotives** used steam pressure from boiling water to turn their wheels.

DID YOU KNOW?
In the days of stagecoaches, a 560-kilometre journey could take 36 hours and 24 changes of horses. Today it would take less than six hours and one tank of petrol.

The first passenger train service began in England in 1825. Soon trains were carrying hundreds of thousands of people wherever iron tracks were laid.

The first motorcars were not built until the late 1890s. Some of the earliest were made in the United States and England, though they were slow and broke down a lot. They looked much like carts with fancy wheels. What most of us would recognize as a motorcar wouldn't come along for several more years.

LEARN MORE! READ THESE ARTICLES...
AIRPLANES · AUTOMOBILES · SHIPS

SEARCH LIGHT

What were the first things used by people to get around?
a) their own feet
b) carts
c) donkeys

Answer: a) their own feet

How Henry Ford Made the American Car

Henry Ford was born near Dearborn, Michigan, U.S., in July 1863. As a boy, he loved to play with watches, clocks, and machines - good experience for the person who would build the first affordable car.

Cars had already been built in Europe when Ford experimented with his first **vehicle** in 1899. It had wheels like a bicycle's and a petrol-powered engine that made it move. It was called a Quadricycle and had only two speeds and no reverse.

Within four years Ford had started the Ford Motor Company. His ideas about making cars would change history.

Car makers at the time used parts others had made and put them all together. Ford's company made each and every part that went into their cars. What's more, they made sure that each kind of part was exactly the same.

In 1908 Ford introduced the Model T car. This car worked well and was not costly. It was a big success, but the company couldn't make them quickly enough to satisfy Henry Ford.

In 1913 he started a large factory that made use of his most important idea: the assembly line. Instead of having workers go from car to car, the cars moved slowly down a line while workers stood in place adding parts to them. Each worker added a different part until a whole car was put together.

This meant more cars could be built more quickly at a lower cost. By 1918 half of all cars in the United States were Model Ts. Ford's company had become the largest automobile manufacturer in the world. And Ford had revolutionized the process of **manufacturing**.

SEARCH LIGHT

True or false? Henry Ford built the very first automobile.

LEARN MORE! READ THESE ARTICLES...
AIRPLANES · OIL · TRANSPORTATION

DID YOU KNOW?
Henry Ford is reported to have once said that his customers could get a Model T in 'any colour they like, as long as it's black'.

Henry Ford's first car was the Quadricycle, seen here with Ford driving. It had only two forward speeds and could not back up.

© Underwood & Underwood/Corbis

Answer: FALSE. Henry Ford built the first inexpensive automobile. Gottlieb Daimler, a German, gets credit for building the very first automobile.

SEARCH LIGHT

What modern machine's name sounds a lot like 'ornithopter', the flapping-wing machine that people tried to fly?

The First Flights

From the earliest times people wanted to fly, but no one knew how. Some people thought it would help if their arms were more like bird wings. So they strapped large feathery wings to their arms. Not one left the ground. A few even tried machines with flapping wings, called 'ornithopters'. These didn't work either.

> ### DID YOU KNOW?
> In 1986 Dick Rutan and Jeana Yeager made the first non-stop round-the-world flight in an airplane. They did the whole trip without refuelling.

Then in 1799 a British scientist named Sir George Cayley wrote a book and drew pictures explaining how birds use their wings and the speed of the wind to fly. About a hundred years later, two American brothers named Orville and Wilbur Wright read Cayley's book. Although they were bicycle makers, they decided to build a flying machine.

The Wright brothers' machine, *Flyer I*, had the strong light wings of a **glider**, a petrol-powered engine, and two **propellers**. Then, from a list of places where strong winds blow, they selected the Kill Devil Hills near Kitty Hawk, North Carolina, U.S., as the site of their experiment.

In 1903 Orville, lying flat on the lower wing of *Flyer I*, flew a distance of 37 metres. That first flight lasted only 12 seconds. The next year the Wrights managed to fly their second 'aeroplane', *Flyer II*, nearly 5 kilometres over a period of 5 minutes and 4 seconds.

Soon Glenn Curtiss, another American bicycle maker, made a faster airplane called the '1909 type'. Not long after that Louis Blériot from France did something no one had tried before. He flew his plane across the English Channel. He was the first man to fly across the sea.

The age of flight had begun.

LEARN MORE! READ THESE ARTICLES…
AUTOMOBILES • SHIPS • WIND POWER

The Wright brothers had read that wind was very important for flying. That's why they chose the windy hill in North Carolina to test their machines.
© Bettmann/Corbis

Answer: How about the 'helicopter'? The '-opter' part of both words means 'wing'. A helicopter's name means 'whirling wing'. An ornithopter's means 'bird wing'.

11

From Rafts to Ocean Liners

We don't know exactly how the first transport over water happened. But it's not hard to imagine how it might have come about.

Long ago, people used anything that would float to move things across water, including bundles of reeds, large jars, and covered baskets.

Perhaps one day someone tied three or four logs together and made a raft. Maybe someone else hollowed out a log as a type of **canoe**. These log boats could be moved by people paddling with their hands. Later they might have used a stick or a pole to make their boat move faster.

Whoever put the first sail on a boat made a wonderful discovery. Sailing was faster and easier than paddling because it caught the wind and used it to move the boat.

SEARCH LIGHT

From each pair, pick the boat that was developed first:
a) raft or sailing boat
b) submarine or canoe
c) paddle steamer or rowing boat

Eventually, someone built a ship that used a sail and long paddles, called 'oars'. When there was little or no wind, the sailors rowed with the oars. In time, sailors learned to turn, or 'set', a sail to make the boat go in almost any direction they wanted.

Later, paddles were used in giant wheels that moved large boats through the water. A steam engine powered these paddle wheels, which were too heavy to turn by hand. Steamboats cruised rivers, lakes, and oceans all over the world.

Today, ships and boats use many different types of engine. Most ships use oil to **generate** power. Some submarines run on nuclear power. But on warm days, many people still enjoy travelling on water by paddling, sailing, and even rafting.

DID YOU KNOW?
In 1947 the Norwegian scientist Thor Heyerdahl and a small crew sailed across more than 8,000 kilometres of ocean on a balsawood raft called the *Kon-Tiki*. It was an experiment to see whether ancient Americans could have settled some Pacific islands.

LEARN MORE! READ THESE ARTICLES...
SUBMARINES • WATER POWER • WIND POWER

Today's ocean liners are a popular way for people to get from one place to another and have a holiday on the way.
© Corbis

Answer: a) raft   b) canoe   c) rowing boat

Silent Stalkers
of the Sea

Because they are meant to spend most of their time underwater, submarines are designed and built quite differently from other ships.

Submarines must be airtight so that water can't get inside them when they **submerge**. They also need to have strong **hulls** because the pressure of seawater at great depths is strong enough to crush ships. And submarines need special engines that don't use air when they are underwater. Otherwise, they would quickly run out of air and shut down! So most modern subs are powered by electric batteries when they're submerged. Some are powered by nuclear energy.

Because a submarine is completely closed up, it must have special instruments to act as its eyes and ears underwater. A periscope is a viewing **device** that can be raised up out of the water to allow the submarine officers to see what is around them. Another special system, sonar, 'hears' what is under the water by sending out sound waves that bounce off everything in their path. These echoes send a sound-picture back to the sub.

But why build submarines in the first place? Well, submarines have been very useful in times of war. They can hide underwater and take enemy ships by surprise.

Submarines have peaceful uses too. Scientists use smaller submarines, called 'submersibles', to explore the huge ocean floors and the creatures that live there. People also use submersibles to search for sunken ships and lost treasure. The luxury liner *Titanic* was discovered and explored with a submersible 73 years after it sank in the Atlantic Ocean.

LEARN MORE! READ THESE ARTICLES...
NUCLEAR ENERGY • RADIO • SHIPS

SEARCH LIGHT

Fill in the gaps: Submarines need _____ that don't use up _____.

DID YOU KNOW?
The *Nautilus*, the first nuclear sub, was once caught by a fishing net. The fishing boat and its unhappy crew were towed for several kilometres before the situation was sorted out.

When a submarine travels above the water, officers can stand on top of the conning tower. This is the raised deck of the ship.
© George Hall/Corbis

Turning Trees to Paper

The pages in your exercise book are made of paper that came from a factory. So are the pages of this book.

The factory got the paper from a paper mill. The mill probably made the paper from logs. And the logs were cut from trees that grew in a forest. Pine trees are often used to make paper.

If you visit a **traditional** paper mill, you will see people working at large noisy machines that peel bark off the logs and then cut the wood into smaller pieces. Other machines press and grind this wood into very tiny pieces that can be mashed together like potatoes. This gooey stuff is called 'wood **pulp**'.

After it is mixed with water, the pulp flows onto a screen where the water drains off, leaving a thin wet sheet of pulp.

Big hot rollers press and then dry this wet pulp as it moves along **conveyor belts**. At the end of the line, the dried pulp comes out as giant rolls of paper. These giant rolls are what the paper factories make into the products that you use every day, such as newspapers, paper towels, and the pages of books that you read.

Because we use so much paper, we must be careful how many trees we cut down to make it. Fortunately, nowadays, a lot of used paper can be remade into new paper by **recycling**. You can help save trees by recycling the magazines, newspapers, and other paper that you use in school and at home.

LEARN MORE! READ THESE ARTICLES...
PHOTOGRAPHY • PRINTING • WEAVING

SEARCH LIGHT

Starting with a tree in a forest, arrange these mixed-up steps in the order they should happen in papermaking: (*Start*) tree → chop down tree, dry, peel bark, roll out sheets, cut up wood, press flat, grind into pulp

In a paper mill like this, the rolls of paper are sometimes as big as the trees they are made from.
© Philip Gould/Corbis

DID YOU KNOW?
According to Chinese historical records, the first paper was made from tree bark, hemp (a plant used to make rope), rags, and fishing nets.

Gutenberg's Gift

SEARCH LIGHT

Why did Gutenberg make the letters on individual pieces of type face backwards? (Hint: Think about looking at writing in a mirror.)

Before about 550 years ago, very few people owned books. In fact, there weren't many books to own. In those days, most books had to be written out by hand. Some books were printed by using wooden blocks with the letters of an entire page hand-carved into each block. The carved side of the block was dipped in ink and pressed onto paper. Both handwritten and woodblock-printed books took a lot of time, energy, and money. Only rich people could afford to buy them.

Then, in the 1450s, a man in Germany named Johannes Gutenberg had an idea for printing books faster.

First, he produced small blocks of metal with one raised backwards-facing letter on each block. These blocks with their raised letters were called 'type'. He then spelled out words and sentences by lining up the individual pieces of type in holders.

The second part of his invention was the printing press. This was basically a 'bed' in which the lines of type could be laid out to create a page. When he inked the lines of type and then used a large plate to press them against a sheet of paper, lines of words were printed on the paper.

Gutenberg's movable type and printing press, unlike carved woodblocks, meant that he could take his lines apart and reuse the letters. Once he had carved enough sets of individual letters, he didn't have to carve new ones to make new pages.

The Bible was one of the earliest books printed by using Gutenberg's movable type. By 1500 the printing presses of Europe had produced about 6 million books!

LEARN MORE! READ THESE ARTICLES...
BRAILLE • PAPER • TELEVISION

DID YOU KNOW?
The Chinese actually invented a kind of movable type 400 years before Gutenberg. But Chinese writing uses thousands of characters and they didn't invent a press, so the invention wasn't a success.

The artist had to imagine Gutenberg and his first page of print. But the printing press in the background is a fairly accurate image of what the inventor worked with.
© Bettmann/Corbis

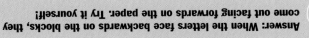

Answer: When the letters face backwards on the blocks, they come out facing forwards on the paper. Try it yourself!

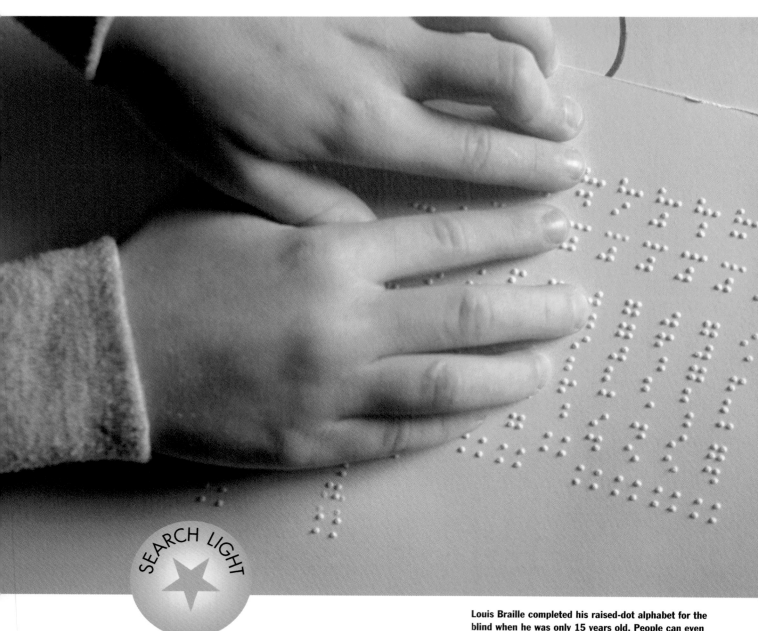

SEARCH LIGHT

Louis Braille invented his Braille alphabet when he was 15. At that age, how many years had he been blind?

Books to Touch

More than 175 years ago in France, a young Louis Braille thought of a way to help blind people read and write. He himself could not see. He had hurt his eyes when he was just 3 years old. He was playing with his father's tools, and one of them blinded him forever.

Fortunately, Louis was a clever child. When he was 10 years old, he won a **scholarship** to the National Institute for Blind Children in Paris.

At the school Louis heard about how Captain Barbier, an army officer, had invented a system of writing that used dots. It was called 'night writing', and it helped soldiers read messages in the dark. These messages were of small bump-like dots pressed on a sheet of paper. The dots were easy to make and could be felt quickly.

Louis decided to use similar dots to make an alphabet for the blind. It was slow to be accepted but eventually was a great success. His alphabet used 63 different dot patterns to represent letters, numbers, punctuation, and several other useful signs. People could even learn to read music by feeling dots.

Today blind people all over the world can learn the Braille alphabet. Look at these dots:

In an actual Braille book, the tips of your fingers would be able to cover each small group of dots.

Can you guess what this pattern of dot letters spells?

It spells the words 'I can read'.

LEARN MORE! READ THESE ARTICLES…
RADIO • PRINTING • SIGHT AND SOUND

DID YOU KNOW?
On their Web site, the American Foundation for the Blind has a great area where you can learn Braille yourself. Go to http://afb.org and click on 'Braille Bug'.

Eyes That Hear, Speech That's Seen

Mary: 'Can you come to the shop with me?'

Sara: 'I'll ask my mother'.

If Mary and Sara were like most girls you know, their conversation would not be unusual. But Mary and Sara are deaf, which means that they can't hear. However, they can understand each other.

How?

Well, one way that people who are deaf communicate is by using sign language. Sign language replaces spoken words with finger and hand movements, **gestures**, and facial expressions. People using sign language can actually talk faster than if they were speaking out loud.

SEARCH LIGHT

This article mentions several ways in which people who are deaf can know what another person is saying. One is lip-reading. What is one of the others?

Deaf child learning to speak using touch, sight, and imitation.
© Nathan Benn/Corbis

Another way people who are deaf may communicate is through lip-reading. People who lip-read have learned to recognize spoken words by reading the shapes and movements speakers make with their lips, mouths, and tongues. Lip-readers usually speak out loud themselves even though they can't hear what others say.

Some people who are deaf use hearing aids or cochlear **implants** to help them hear the sounds and words that others hear. (The cochlea is part of the ear.) Hearing aids usually fit outside the ear and make sounds louder. Cochlear implants are inside the ear and use electrical signals to imitate sounds for the brain. Often children and adults with hearing aids or implants have lessons to learn to speak as hearing people do.

There are many schools for children who are deaf or hearing-**impaired**. There they may learn all or some of the skills of lip-reading, sign language, **oral** speech, and the use of hearing aids and implants. Older students may attend Gallaudet University in Washington, D.C., U.S., a university especially for people who are deaf.

LEARN MORE! READ THESE ARTICLES…
BRAILLE • INTERNET • TELEPHONES

Many deaf children learn to communicate by using sign language.
© Mug Shots/Corbis

DID YOU KNOW?
Some famous people have been deaf:
Juliette Gordon Low, who founded the
Girl Scouts; 1995 Miss America
Heather Whitestone; and LeRoy
Colombo, who, as a lifeguard, saved
907 people.

Answer: In addition to lip-reading, sign language allows many deaf
people to communicate. And some deaf people use hearing aids
or implants to help them hear sound and spoken language.

Staying in Touch

The telephone is the most popular communication **device** of all time.

Alexander Graham Bell invented the telephone in 1876. In 11 years there were more than 150,000 telephones in the United States and 26,000 in the United Kingdom. In 2001 there were an estimated 1,400,000,000 telephones worldwide.

Traditional telephones have three main parts: a **transmitter**, a receiver, and a dialler. There is also a switch hook, which hangs up and disconnects the call.

When you speak into the phone, the transmitter changes the sound of your voice into an electrical signal. The transmitter is basically a tiny **microphone** in the mouthpiece. On the other end of the call, the receiver in the listener's earpiece changes that electrical signal back into sound. The receiver is a tiny vibrating disk, and the electrical signal vibrates the disk to make the sounds of the caller's voice.

When you make a call, the phone's dialler sends a series of clicks or tones to a switching office. On a rotating dial phone, dialling the number 3 causes three clicks to interrupt the normal sound on the line (the dial tone). On a touchtone phone, a pushed number interrupts the dial tone with a new sound. These interruptions are a form of code. The telephone exchange 'reads' the code and sends the call to the right telephone receiver.

Since the 1990s, mobile phones have become hugely popular worldwide. Mobile phones connect with small transmitter-receivers that each control an area, or 'cell'. As a person moves from one cell to the next, the mobile phone switches the signal it receives to the new cell.

LEARN MORE! READ THESE ARTICLES...
INTERNET • RADIO • SIGHT AND SOUND

SEARCH LIGHT

A telephone receiver is a
a) vibrating disk.
b) dial tone.
c) tiny microphone.

DID YOU KNOW?

Deaf and hard-of-hearing people can use telephone-like devices that turn their typed message into sound and the other person's voice into type. One such device is a TTY (for *TeleTYpes*), and another is a TDD (Telecommunications Device for the Deaf).

SEARCH LIGHT

Find and
correct the
mistake in the
following sentence:
A set of instructions
that a computer uses
to solve problems
and do work is called
'memory'.

The Machines That Solve Problems

The first computers were expensive room-sized machines that only business and government offices could afford. Today most computers are smaller, and many people have one in their own home or school. These 'personal computers' (PCs) first appeared in the mid-1970s.

A Palm Pilot, one of the tiny but powerful modern computers.
© RNT Productions/Corbis

Computers can find the answers to many maths problems and can simplify work that has many steps and would otherwise take lots of time. They can do this because they can remember, in order, the individual steps of even long and complicated instructions.

The sets of instructions for computers are called 'programs' or 'software'. A computer's brain is its microprocessor - a tiny electronic **device** that reads and carries out the program's instructions.

Because they are programmed in advance, you can use computers to solve maths problems, remember facts, and play games. Computers can also help you draw, write essays, and make your own greeting cards.

Computers need two kinds of memory. 'Main memory' is what handles the information that the computer is using as it is doing its work. Main memory operates amazingly fast and powerfully to speed up a computer's work. The second kind of computer memory is **storage** for its programs and for the results of its operations. The most important storage space is on the computer's hard drive, or hard disk. CD-ROMs and floppy disks are removable storage devices.

Since 1990 very small computers have been developed. Today there are laptop or notebook computers, as well as handheld computers. Handheld computers weigh only a few grams, but they can handle more **data** more quickly that most of the first giant computers.

LEARN MORE! READ THESE ARTICLES…
ELECTRICITY • INTERNET • PRINTING

DID YOU KNOW?
It was a weaving machine, a loom, that led to the first computers. At one time, looms used punched cards to set weaving patterns. Early computers used this system of coding in their 'programming languages'.

Answer: A set of instructions that a computer uses to solve problems and do work is called a 'program' [or 'software'].

27

Network of People

You can do things with your friends and family even when they are thousands of kilometres away simply by sitting at your computer. The Internet makes this possible.

As the name suggests, the Internet is like a large net whose every strand connects to a different computer. It is an international web linking millions of computer users around the world. Together with the World Wide Web (WWW, or Web), it is used for sending and receiving e-mail and for sharing information on almost any topic.

The Web is an enormous electronic library from which anyone connected to the Internet can receive information. It is organised into tens of millions of sites, each identified by an electronic address called the 'uniform resource locator' (URL). The Web allows you to view photographs and films, listen to songs and hear people speak, and find out about **countless** different things you never knew before.

The Internet has come a long way since 1969, when it all began. At that time the U.S. Defense Department was testing **methods** of making their computers survive a military attack. Soon their networks were extended to various research computers around the United States and then to countries around the world.

By early 1990 the Internet and the World Wide Web had entered homes. Today many people wonder how they ever managed without the Internet.

LEARN MORE! READ THESE ARTICLES...
COMPUTERS • RADIO • TELEPHONES

DID YOU KNOW?
Radio took about 38 years to gain 50 million listeners. TV took about 13 years to have 50 million viewers. The Internet took only 4 years to get 50 million users.

SEARCH LIGHT

The Internet is more than
a) 10 years old.
b) 20 years old.
c) 30 years old.

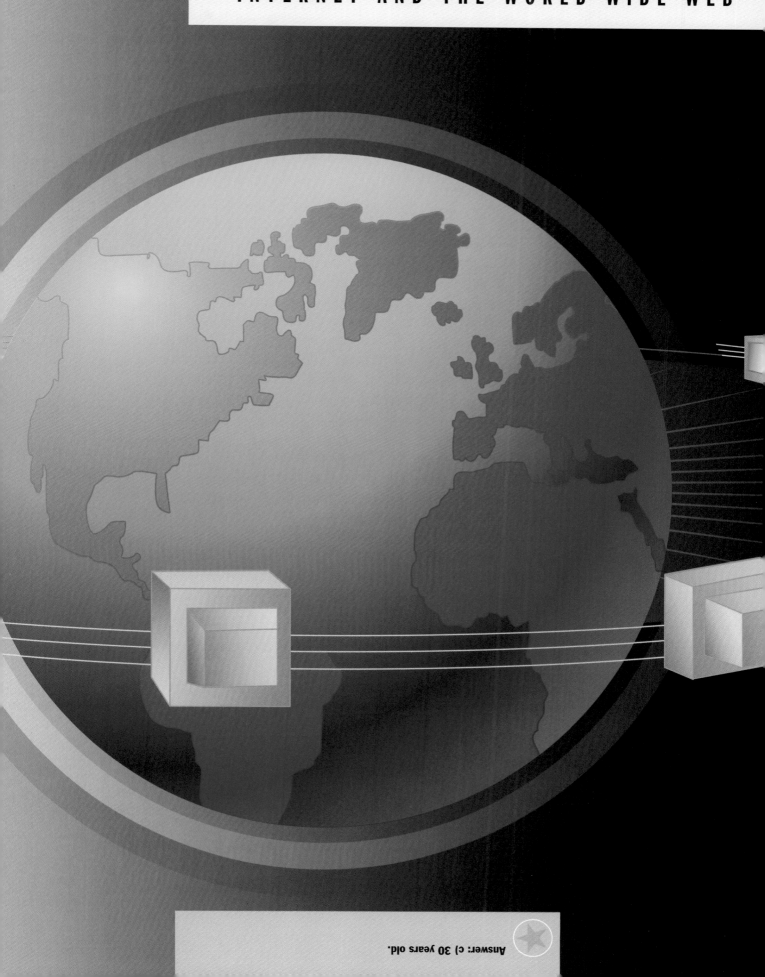

Cables, Fuses, Wires, and Energy

You can't see electricity, but you know it's there when you watch an electric light go on, hear the telephone ring, or watch the television.

Electricity comes into your house through thick wires called 'cables'. These join a **fuse** box. From the fuse box run all the electric wires for your house. Each wire connects to a plug socket or a switch. From there, electricity passes along the plugs and leads that go into an appliance, lamp, or television.

Electricity moves easily along things made of metal, such as silver, copper, or iron. That's why copper wires are used to carry the electricity. Electricity doesn't pass through rubber or plastic. That's why wires carrying electricity are usually coated with rubber or plastic.

This coating is important, because electricity will flow wherever it can. When it is loose, it can be very dangerous. It can cause shocks, start fires, or even kill.

Did you know that electricity can be used to make a magnet? If a wire is wound into a coil and wrapped around a piece of iron, the iron will become a magnet when electricity is sent through the coil. The iron will then attract other things made of iron and steel. Such a magnet is called an 'electromagnet'.

As soon as the electricity is turned off, the electromagnet isn't a magnet anymore. If the magnet is holding something when the electricity is turned off, that thing will drop.

LEARN MORE! READ THESE ARTICLES...
TELEPHONES • WATER POWER • WIND POWER

SEARCH LIGHT

Fill in the gaps:
To prevent shocks, electric wires should be wrapped with _____ or _____.

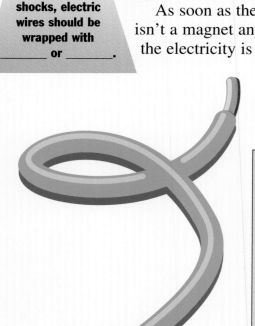

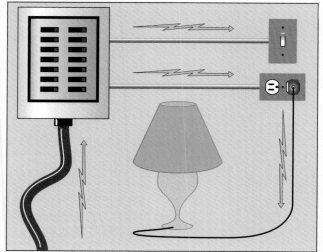

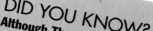

DID YOU KNOW?
Although Thomas Edison is better
known for his light bulb, films, and
phonograph, his first invention was
an electric voting machine.

Answer: To prevent shocks, electric wires should be wrapped with
rubber or plastic.

Hundreds of wind turbines like these in Denmark are set up on 'wind farms' in constantly windy areas to produce large amounts of electricity.
© Adam Woolfitt/Corbis

SEARCH LIGHT

Which of the following are advantages of wind power? It's inexpensive. It works everywhere. It's clean. It's endless.

DID YOU KNOW?
The total wind power of our atmosphere, at any one time, is estimated to be 3.6 billion kilowatts. That's enough energy to light 36 billion light bulbs all at once.

Energy in the Air

Wind power has been used for many hundreds of years. Its energy has filled the sails of ships and powered machines that grind grain, pump water, drain marshes, saw wood, and make paper. Wind provides a clean and endless source of energy.

In the 1890s windmills in Denmark became the first to use wind power to generate electricity. But it took the major energy crisis of the 1970s to focus people's thoughts seriously again on using wind energy to produce electricity.

Traditional windmills in the Netherlands.
© ML Sinibaldi/Corbis

Windmills provide power to make electricity when their sails are turned by wind blowing against them. Originally, the sails were long narrow sheets of canvas stretched over a wooden frame. Later windmills used different materials and designs. Usually there are four sails shaped like large blades.

When the sails turn, the axle they are attached to turns as well, much as car wheels turn on their axles. The axle causes various **gears** to turn, which then causes a large crankshaft to turn. The crankshaft is a long pole running the length of the windmill tower. At its other end the crankshaft is attached to a generator, a motor that can make and store electricity. So when the wind blows, the generator runs - making electricity.

Today, modern efficient wind machines called 'wind turbines' are used to generate electricity. These machines have from one to four blades and operate at high speeds. The first of these wind turbines appeared in the mid-1990s.

LEARN MORE! READ THESE ARTICLES...
ELECTRICITY · SHIPS · WATER POWER

Answer: Wind power is inexpensive, clean, and endless. Unfortunately, it's not a usable way to generate power in areas with little or no wind.

Energy from Heat

Energy means power - the power to do work. And thermal, or heat, energy can do a lot of work. When heat is applied to water, for instance, it makes the water boil. Boiling water then changes to vapour, or steam, which can apply great force as it escapes a container. Large quantities of steam powered the earliest train engines.

The most important source of thermal energy for our Earth is the Sun's rays. This '**solar** energy' is used to heat houses, water,

© Keren Su/Corbis

© Paul A. Souders,/Corbis

(Top) Sun's heat focussed and used for cooking on solar oven by Tibetan monk. **(Bottom)** Locomotive fireman shovels coal to burn, boiling water to produce steam power.

and, in some countries, ovens used for cooking. Solar power can even be **converted** to electricity and stored for later use.

To people, the second most important source of thermal energy is the store of natural fuels on and in the Earth. When these fuels (mainly coal, oil, gas, and wood) are burned, they produce heat. This heat can be used for warmth, made to power a machine directly, or converted into electricity. For example, a car engine burns petroleum (an oil product) for direct thermal power. In some areas, coal is burned to produce the electricity that powers people's homes.

In a very few parts of the world, an interesting third form of heat energy comes from 'living' heat inside the Earth itself. This 'geothermal energy' comes from such sources as natural hot springs and the heat of active volcanoes ('geo-' means 'earth'). Naturally escaping steam and hot water are used to heat and power homes and businesses in Reykjavik, Iceland. And though volcanoes are mostly too hot to tap directly, worldwide experiments continue as other major fuel supplies **dwindle**.

LEARN MORE! READ THESE ARTICLES...
AUTOMOBILES • ELECTRICITY • OIL

© Raymond Gehman/Corbis

The intense power of the Earth's heat energy sometimes bursts into geysers - hot springs that send roaring columns of steam and boiling water high above the surface. This geyser is the famous Old Faithful in Yellowstone National Park in Wyoming, U.S.

DID YOU KNOW?

Hot-air ballooning, a popular sport in the 1960s, relies on thermal power. A gas burner heats air that is then fed into a large airtight balloon. And because hot air rises, the balloon rises up and away - carrying people or cargo along in its basket or container.

Answer: When steam escapes, it gives a mighty push. This push is so strong that it was used to move the early train engines.

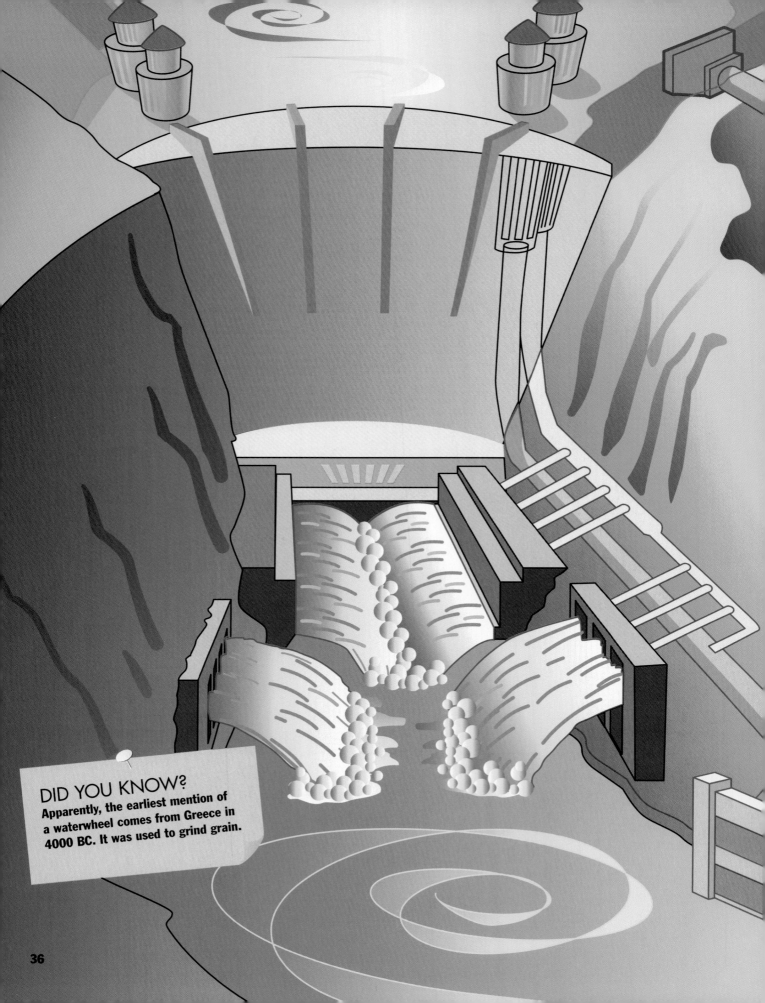

DID YOU KNOW?
Apparently, the earliest mention of a waterwheel comes from Greece in 4000 BC. It was used to grind grain.

Streams of Energy

We have only to hear the roar of a waterfall to guess at the power of water. Its force is also clear anytime we see the damage caused by floods. But the water power can be extremely useful as well as destructive.

One excellent aspect of water power is that the water can be reused. Unlike such fuels as coal and oil, water does not get used up when **harnessed** for power. And it doesn't pollute the air either.

The power of water lies not in the water itself but in the flow of water. The power produced by water depends upon the water's

© Hubert Stadler/Corbis

weight and its height of fall, called 'head'. Generally, the faster that water moves, the more power it can generate. That's why water flowing from a higher place to a lower place, as a waterfall does, can produce so much energy.

Since ancient times people have used the energy of water to grind wheat and other grains.

They first **devised** the waterwheel, a wheel with paddles around its rim. As the photograph shows, the wheel was mounted on a frame over a river. The flowing water striking the blades turned the wheel.

Later, larger waterwheels were used to run machines in factories. They were not very reliable, however. Floodwaters could create too much power, whereas long rainless periods left the factories without any power at all.

Today, streamlined metal waterwheels called 'turbines' help produce electricity. The electricity produced by water is called 'hydroelectric power' ('hydro-' means 'water'). Enormous dams, like the one pictured here, provide this **superior** source of electricity.

LEARN MORE! READ THESE ARTICLES…
ELECTRICITY • SHIPS • THERMAL POWER

Big Energy
from a Small Source

All **matter** is made up of tiny particles called 'molecules'. In turn, all molecules are made up of even tinier particles called 'atoms'.

The central part of an atom is called a 'nucleus'. When the nucleus splits in two, it produces enormous energy. This breaking apart is called 'nuclear fission'. If two nuclei join and form a bigger nucleus - in a process called 'nuclear fusion' - even more energy is produced.

The nuclear energy released from fission and fusion is called 'radiation'. Radiation - the process of giving off **rays** - is a powerful spreading of heat, light, sound, or even invisible beams.

SEARCH LIGHT

What is the main problem with nuclear energy?

One of the first uses of nuclear energy was to build deadly weapons. Atomic bombs built during World War II and dropped on Hiroshima and Nagasaki in Japan largely destroyed those cities and killed many thousands of people. People worldwide now try to make sure that this will never happen again.

Today, however, nuclear energy has many helpful uses. Nuclear power plants produce low-cost electricity. Nuclear energy also fuels submarines. And it has also allowed doctors to see more details inside the body than ever before.

But nuclear energy has its **drawbacks**. Nuclear energy produces nuclear waste. Living beings exposed to the waste can suffer from radiation poisoning. They may experience damaged blood and organs, effects that can be deadly. And the radiation can remain active for thousands of years wherever nuclear waste is thrown away.

Unfortunately, no country has yet discovered the perfect way to store nuclear waste. But the benefits make it worthwhile to keep trying.

LEARN MORE! READ THESE ARTICLES...
SUBMARINES • THERMAL POWER • WATER POWER

DID YOU KNOW?
We all actually enjoy the benefits of nuclear energy every day. The Sun, like all stars, is simply a giant nuclear power plant. Its heat and light are the products of nuclear energy.

Nuclear power plant on the coast of California, U.S.
© Galen Rowell/Corbis

Answer: Nuclear energy produces poisonous waste that remains deadly for generations. No one has yet come up with a safe and highly reliable way to get rid of the waste.

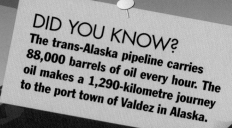

From the Ground
to the Petrol Station

Up comes the thick black oil from the oil well and...out pours the petrol into your family's car. But how does the oil become fuel for vehicles?

Petroleum, or crude oil, is oil as it is found deep within the Earth. This raw form has many unwanted substances in it that must eventually be removed in a process called 'refining'.

From wells drilled deep into the ground, the oil often goes through long underground pipelines. There are pipelines in some very surprising places - under streets, mountains, deserts, frozen lands, and even lakes and rivers.

Pumping stations keep the thick oil moving through the pipes. Each station gives the oil enough of a push for it to reach the next station. There are pumping stations built all along the pipelines. Here and there along the pipelines, oil is directed into smaller pipes that take it to huge storage tanks.

From the storage tanks, the oil goes to a **refinery**, where it is heated until it is very hot. The hot oil is separated into many different substances. The heavy part that settles down at the bottom is used for road building. Other parts become machine oils and waxes. **Paraffin** and petrol also separate as the oil is heated. Finally, the lightest parts of the oil - cooking gas and other types of gas - are collected.

From the refineries, more pipelines carry oil to round storage tanks in tank farms. Petrol tankers fill up at the storage tanks and take the fuel to petrol stations, where people can fill the tanks in their cars.

LEARN MORE! READ THESE ARTICLES...
AUTOMOBILES • POLLUTION • THERMAL ENERGY

SEARCH LIGHT

Put the different stages in the correct order, beginning with the oil well. (Start) oil well → *pipelines, petrol station, pipelines, refinery, storage tank, pumping station*

888.88

Answer: oil well → pipelines → pumping station → storage tank → refinery → pipelines → petrol station

DID YOU KNOW?
It's estimated that the energy saved by recycling just one glass bottle would light up a light bulb for four hours.

Harming Our Environment

Have you ever seen black smoke pouring out of factory chimneys, turning the sky a dirty grey colour? This is air pollution. Cars, lorries, buses, and even lawnmowers release gases and particles that pollute the air too. Smoke from fires and barbeques also pollutes the air.

Land pollution, water pollution, and even noise pollution are also big problems. Factories and ordinary people may thoughtlessly dump rubbish and **waste** on land or in water. And when farm chemicals that kill insect pests or help crops grow sink into the ground and water, they pollute too. And noise pollution is created by loud machines and honking horns.

Ocean life isn't safe from pollution. The picture you see here shows a crew cleaning up a polluted seashore after an oil spill. Ships carrying petroleum sometimes have accidents, and their oil spills into the ocean.

Dirty air, land, and water are dangerous. Dirty air, or **smog**, is hard to breathe and makes people and animals sick. Dirty water makes people and animals sick when they drink it or wash or live in it. It also kills plants. If land takes in too much waste, nothing will grow on it and it becomes unfit to live on.

Stopping pollution isn't easy. Most people find it hard to change the way they live, even if they want to. And governments and big companies find it even harder to change, since the changes are often unpopular or expensive.

Even small changes help, however. Reusing things instead of throwing them away helps. Using less water every day helps. So does **recycling**. And perhaps in the future people will use cleaner forms of energy, such as wind power and solar energy.

LEARN MORE! READ THESE ARTICLES...
AUTOMOBILES • NUCLEAR ENERGY • WIND POWER

SEARCH LIGHT

Match each item to the kind of pollution it creates.

litter	air
smog	land
oil spill	noise
car honking	water

Answer: litter = *land*   smog = *air*
oil spill = *water*   car honking = *noise*

Making Cloth

'Shu-dul-ig! Shu-dul-og!'

The shuttle in this weaver's left hand flies back and forth, carrying its thread.

A shuttle is part of a loom, a machine that makes cloth. Cloth is composed of threads crisscrossing each other.

'Warp' threads run up and down lengthwise on the loom. The shuttle carries the 'weft' thread back and forth, passing it over and under the sets of warp thread. This is how simple cloth like muslin is woven. Making patterned and other complicated cloth is a more complex weaving process.

The threads for weaving cloth are made of fibres - thin, wispy strands often tangled together. Some fibres come from animals, some from plants, and some from synthetic (artificial) sources. Fine silk fibres come from the cocoon of a silkworm - actually the caterpillar stage of a moth. People learned to spin fibres into threads a very long time ago.

The most commonly used animal fibre is wool. Most wool is the hair of sheep, but some comes from goats, camels, llamas, and several other animals. Woollen cloth keeps you nice and warm when it's cold outside.

Cotton is a plant fibre. Some cotton fibres are so thin that just about half a kilo of them can be spun into a thread about 160 kilometres long! Work clothing and summer clothes are often made of cotton.

Fine silk cloth is shiny and smooth. It is more expensive than cotton because silkworms need a lot of care. And each silkworm makes only a small amount of silk.

Today, weaving by hand has become mostly a specialized **craft**. As with much other manufacturing, modern cloth is usually produced by machines.

SEARCH LIGHT

Which of the following descriptions matches the term 'weft'?
a) cross threads
b) up-and-down threads
c) weaving machine
d) source of silk

LEARN MORE! READ THESE ARTICLES...
BRAILLE • COMPUTERS • MEASUREMENT

DID YOU KNOW?
The strongest piece of weaving anywhere is a spider web. One strand of spider silk is thought to be stronger than an equal-sized piece of steel.

SEARCH LIGHT

What was probably the earliest use for calendars?

Charting the Year

A calendar, like a clock, provides a way to count time - though calendars count days and months rather than minutes and hours. The modern calendar has 12 months of 30 or 31 days each (February has 28, sometimes 29). The calendar year has 365 days, which is about how long it takes the Earth to circle the Sun once. That makes it a **solar** calendar.

Today's calendar, with a few changes, has been in use since 1582. Pope Gregory XIII had it designed to correct errors in the previous calendar. For this reason it is called the 'Gregorian calendar'.

The oldest calendars were used to work out when to plant, harvest, and store crops. These were often '**lunar** calendars', based on the number of days it took the Moon to appear full and then **dwindle** away again.

Jewish calendar (in Hebrew) from the 1800s.
© Archivo Iconografico, S.A./Corbis

DID YOU KNOW?
The Chinese calendar names each year for one of 12 animals. In order, these are: rat, ox, tiger, hare, dragon, snake, horse, sheep, monkey, fowl, dog, and pig. The year 2003 is the Year of the Sheep (or Ram), 2004 the Year of the Monkey, and so on.

The traditional Chinese calendar is a lunar calendar. It has 354 days, with months of either 29 or 30 days.

Many calendars have religious origins. In Central and South America, the ancient Aztec and Mayan calendars marked **ritual** days and celebrations. Jews, Muslims, and Hindus have religious calendars - each with a different number of days and months.

All these calendars have one thing in common: they're wrong. None of them measures the Earth's yearlong journey around the Sun precisely. Extra days must be added to keep the count in step with the actual seasons. We add an extra day to February every four years. (Actually, even our corrections are wrong. Once every 400 years we *don't* add that day.)

But if we didn't make some kind of correction, we'd eventually have New Year's Eve in the middle of the year!

LEARN MORE! READ THESE ARTICLES...
COMPUTERS · MEASUREMENT · PRINTING

This ancient Aztec calendar stone weighs about 25 tons. Its central image of the Aztec sun god, Tonatiuh, indicates the important role religion plays in how major civilizations measure time.
© Randy Faris/Corbis

Answer: The earliest calendars were likely used to tell the right time to plant and harvest crops.

A NASA probe to Mars ended up crashing because the two teams of scientists working on it used different measurement systems. One team used metric and the other used the Imperial system, so directions given to the probe sent it too close to the planet.

SEARCH LIGHT

Guess which unit of measure was originally defined as equal to 'an average throwing stone'.
a) a pound
b) a cup
c) an inch

Understanding Size and Distance

How far away from you is the nearest chair? You can make your own measurement to find out how many shoes away the chair is.

Stand up where you are and face the chair. Count 'one' for your right shoe. Now place the heel of your left shoe against the toe of your right shoe and count 'two'. Continue stepping, heel-to-toe, right then left, counting each shoe length, until you get to the chair.

Centuries ago, people did just what you are doing now. They used parts of the body to measure things. An inch was about the width of a man's thumb. A foot was the length of his foot. A yard was the distance from the tip of his nose to the end of his thumb when his arm was stretched out. But since everyone's thumbs, feet, and arms were different sizes, so were everyone's inches, feet, and yards!

Finally, in the 1800s, all these terms were standardised - that is, everyone in England agreed on a specific definition for each one. They became part of the English system of measurement, called the British **Imperial** System.

We also use another system, called the 'metric system'. This measures in centimetres and metres, grams and kilograms, and litres. All these measurements can be multiplied or divided by 10. Fortunately, most of the world accepts the metric system or the Imperial system as the **standard** of measurement. So, we know today that one measurement will mean the same thing, no matter where it is used or who's doing the measuring.

LEARN MORE! READ THESE ARTICLES...
AUTOMOBILES · CALENDAR · COMPUTERS

6
5
4
3
2
1

Answer: a) a pound. Though people agreed on a pound as the weight of 'an average throwing stone,' there were actually as many different 'pounds' as there were people!

Drawing with Light

The word 'photography' comes from two ancient Greek words: *photo*, for 'light', and *graph*, for 'writing' or 'drawing'.

Photography, the process of taking pictures, requires a camera. But a camera may be any dark lightproof box with a small opening at one end that lets in light. Most cameras have glass **lenses** to help focus the light into the back of the box on the section that holds the film.

Cameras work basically as our eyes do. Light enters the front and shines a picture on the back.

In your eye, light enters through an opening called the 'pupil'. The camera's opening is its aperture. Your iris controls how much light enters your eye. The camera's shutter does the same. In eyes and in most cameras, the light then passes through a lens. In your eye, the picture is

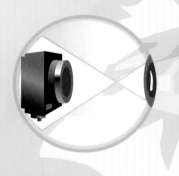

SEARCH LIGHT

Match the parts of the camera to the similar parts of an eye:

1. pupil   a) lens
2. iris   b) film
3. lens   c) shutter
4. retina   d) aperture

produced on the retina, the back lining of the eye. In a camera, the film receives and captures the image.

Photographic film is special material that has been treated with chemicals to make it **sensitive** to light. Light shining on film changes the film's chemical makeup. Depending on how much light shines on each part of the film, different shades or colours result.

Finally, in photography, developing the film creates the photograph. Film that has been exposed to light is processed with chemicals that **fix** the image on special paper.

Today, digital cameras don't use film. Instead, they translate the image into numbers recorded on a disk inside the camera. A personal computer decodes these numbers and displays a picture.

LEARN MORE! READ THESE ARTICLES…
MOTION PICTURES · PRINTING · SIGHT AND SOUND

DID YOU KNOW?

The first photograph - a farmhouse with some fruit trees - was taken in about 1826 by a French inventor, Joseph Nicéphore Niépce.

Photos That Move

Sitting in a darkened cinema, caught up in the adventures of Harry Potter and Hermione Granger, you might find it difficult to believe that you're watching a series of still photographs. These still photos are projected onto the screen so fast, one after another, that you're tricked into seeing movement. This is why early on they were called 'motion pictures' or 'movies'.

Film for shooting cinema comes in long wound **spools** or **cartridges**. The film takes pictures at either 18 or 24 shots per second. Sometimes there are three or four cameras that shoot a scene from different angles. Sound is recorded at the same time but with separate equipment.

Later, the film is **edited** by cutting out parts that the director doesn't want. The parts being kept are then put together to tell the story. The

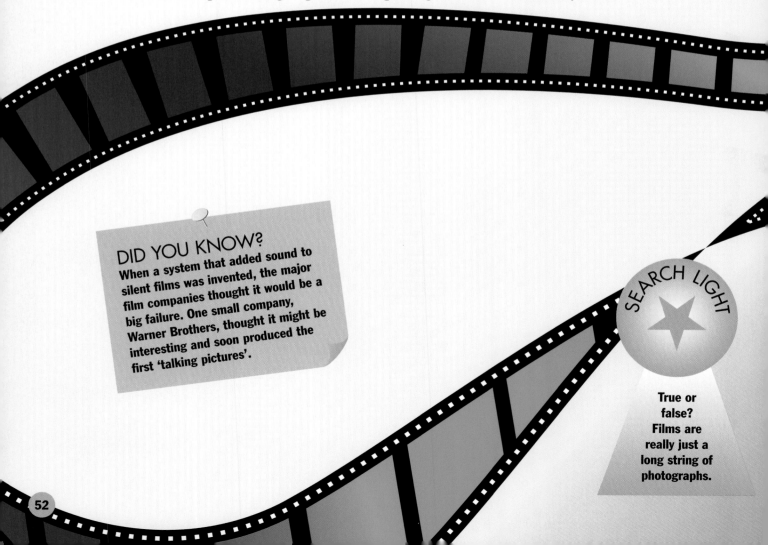

DID YOU KNOW?

When a system that added sound to silent films was invented, the major film companies thought it would be a big failure. One small company, Warner Brothers, thought it might be interesting and soon produced the first 'talking pictures'.

SEARCH LIGHT

True or false? Films are really just a long string of photographs.

finished film, with the sound and the pictures joined together, is shown as a continuous piece.

Film-making is a long and complicated process, involving many people. The actors are the most visible, but there are many others as well. The director has total control over how the story is filmed. A whole crew of people help with costumes, choreography, lighting, sound, camera operations, special effects, and the actors' makeup and hairstyles.

After the film has been shot, there are different people to edit it and other people who advertise the movie. Finally, the film reaches the cinemas. There you buy your popcorn or other refreshments and settle into your seat to enjoy the magic world of the finished film.

LEARN MORE! READ THESE ARTICLES...
PHOTOGRAPHY • RADIO • TELEVISION

Answer: TRUE. When the string of photos is flashed by quickly, the pictures appear to move.

Guglielmo Marconi, seen here in 1922, received the 1909 Nobel Prize for Physics for his development of a way to send electronic signals without using wires.

SEARCH LIGHT

Fill in the gap: After World War I, radio developed from a two-way communication tool into a popular instrument for _____.

Thank You, Mr Marconi

Before there was television, people got much of their news and entertainment from the radio. And many still do!

Invention of the radio began in 1896 when the Italian scientist Guglielmo Marconi **patented** a wireless **telegraph** process. Marconi knew that energy can travel in invisible waves through the air and that these waves can be captured electronically to send and receive signals. His invention allowed people to send messages to each other over great distances without having to be connected by wires.

A Marconi wireless telegraph set (1912), the 'parent' of the voice-transmitting radio.
© Underwood & Underwood/Corbis

Marconi and others added to his invention, working out how to add sound to these messages to make the first radios. These were used simply for sending and receiving messages. During World War I the armed forces used radios for this purpose. It was after the war that radio became popular as a means of entertainment.

During the 1920s radio stations were set up all over the world. In the early days, most of the radio programmes gave news or **broadcast** lectures and some music. As more and more people started to listen to the radio, more popular entertainment programmes were added. These included comedies, dramas, game shows, mysteries, soap operas, and shows for children.

Radio shows remained very popular until the 1950s. That's when television began to catch on. As it happens, television actually works in the same basic ways that radio does! It uses special equipment to send and receive pictures and sound in the form of electronic signals.

Today, radio **technology** is used in many ways. Cordless telephones, mobile phones, and garage-door openers all use radio technology. And radio entertainment programmes are still going strong.

LEARN MORE! READ THESE ARTICLES...
ELECTRICITY • TELEPHONES • TELEVISION

Answer: After World War I, radio developed from a two-way communication tool into a popular instrument for entertainment.

55

The World in a Box

SEARCH LIGHT

True or false? In the beginning most people weren't very interested in the new invention known as 'television'.

The British Broadcasting Corporation (BBC) offered the first public television (TV) programming in 1936. But World War II stalled the development and popularity of the new invention.

At first, people preferred radio to the small, fuzzy black and white pictures and poor sound of early TV. Very few people could even receive the programmes. In the United States, when the 1947 World Series of baseball was shown on TV, many Americans watched and afterward decided to buy TV sets. The turning point in Great Britain came with the televised coronation of Queen Elizabeth II in 1953.

The first TV programmes - mostly news reports, comedies, variety shows, soap operas, and dramas - were based on popular radio shows. Gradually, detective programmes, game shows, sports, films, and children's programmes joined the line-up.

In some countries, independent businesses called 'networks' - groups of stations linked together - choose TV programming and make money by selling advertising time. In other countries, people buy a TV and radio licence, which helps pay for government-sponsored programming. Another system, called 'cable TV', often sells subscriptions that allow viewers to watch their shows.

Broadcast TV works much as radio does. Special equipment changes images and sound into electrical signals. These signals are sent through the air and are received by individual **aerials**, which pass the signals on to the TV sets. There they are read and changed back into images and sound.

The TV technology keeps changing. Colour TV became popular in the mid-1960s, and cable TV and videocassette recorders (VCRs) spread during the '80s. Today, advances such as digital videodiscs (DVDs), high-definition TV, and satellite dishes provide even better picture and sound.

Earth-orbiting satellites have improved TV broadcasting. In fact, the only things that haven't changed much are the kinds of shows people watch and enjoy!

LEARN MORE! READ THESE ARTICLES...
ELECTRICITY · MOTION PICTURES · RADIO

Big-screen TV and video recording have made the viewing experience very different from TV's early days. Now we can watch ourselves on TV!

© Jose Luis Pelaez, Inc./Corbis

Answer: TRUE. Early TV had poor picture and sound quality, and people preferred to listen to radio and use their imaginations.

57

Looking to Nature for Remedies

Two visitors watched a jaguar fall off its tree limb and lie quietly on the ground. Their guide in this South American forest had brought the cat down with a blowgun dart tipped with curare. Made from certain trees in the jungle, curare **paralyses** the muscles in the body.

When scientists heard about this remarkable poison, they experimented with it. Although large doses of curare are deadly, they found that tiny doses can help people relax during **surgery**.

Many years ago, a doctor might have treated stomach-ache with a medicine containing a pinch of gold dust, a spoonful of ash from a dried lizard, 20 powdered beetles, some burned cat's hair, and two mashed onions!

Not all the old recipes for medicine were as bad as this one. Usually medicines were made from tree bark and leaves, berries and seeds, roots, and flowers. The value of some 'folk remedies' has not been proved scientifically, but many modern drugs have been developed from plants, animals, and **minerals**.

The photograph, for example, shows a common flower called 'foxglove'. Its leaves are used to make 'digitalis', which helps people with heart disease. Pods of the opium poppy are used to make painkillers.

Not so long ago, a very important medicine was discovered in mouldy bread. This medicine, penicillin, and others like it are called 'antibiotics'. They help fight many diseases by killing **bacteria**.

Today, most medicines are synthesized. This means that they are made from combinations of chemicals rather than from plants or animals. This method is much more **economical** and allows scientists to create much larger supplies of important medicines.

SEARCH LIGHT

Find and correct the mistake in the following sentence: Many medicines today still come from the bark of animals.

LEARN MORE! READ THESE ARTICLES...
NUCLEAR ENERGY • POLLUTION • TRANSPORTATION

DID YOU KNOW?
Deadly nightshade is a highly poisonous plant that was often used in small amounts as a medicine. It is closely related to the tomato.

Answer: Many medicines today still come from the bark of trees.

Exploring the Sky

The stars we see in the night sky look like little points of light. But they are vastly larger than they look. Almost all of them are much bigger than our Earth. The stars look tiny because they're very far away. If you rode in the fastest rocket for your entire life, you wouldn't make it even halfway to the closest star.

Fortunately, telescopes let us explore the stars without leaving the Earth.

A simple telescope is tube-shaped and has a special kind of **magnifying** glass, called a '**lens**', at each end. Other telescopes use mirrors or both lenses and mirrors to enlarge the faraway view. Lenses and mirrors gather the light from an object, making it seem brighter and easier to see.

Telescopes make stars and planets seem closer. And telescopes let us see much farther than we normally can. Through a simple telescope you can see the rings of the planet Saturn, as well as galaxies outside our own Milky Way. Giant telescopes on mountaintops can view objects much farther away and see with much greater detail. Their lenses and mirrors are often enormous and therefore enormously powerful.

Some modern telescopes don't even look like the ones most of us might look through. These devices, which must travel into space beyond Earth's atmosphere, can sense light and other **radiation** that's invisible to unaided human eyes. These sensitive instruments, such as the Infrared Space Observatory and the Hubble Space Telescope (pictured here), have shown scientists such wonders as the dust in space between galaxies and the births and deaths of stars.

LEARN MORE! READ THESE ARTICLES...
PHOTOGRAPHY • RADIO • SUBMARINES

> **DID YOU KNOW?**
> Special radio telescopes 'listen' to the radio signals produced by stars, galaxies, and other objects. One group in New Mexico, U.S., includes 27 'dish' antennas spread over 40 kilometres.

SEARCH LIGHT

Find and correct the mistake in the following sentence: Telescopes make faraway objects seem faster than they look with the unaided eye.

Behind the Hubble Space Telescope, you can see the Earth's atmosphere outlined.
NASA

 Answer: Telescopes make faraway objects seem closer than they look with the unaided eye.

61

aerial metallic rod or wire for sending or receiving radio waves or other energy signals

bacterium (plural: bacteria) tiny one-celled organism too small to see with the unaided eye

broadcast send out a programme or message to a group, usually by radio, television, or the Internet

canoe a small light and narrow boat having sharp front and back ends and moved by paddling

cartridge sealed container

convert change

conveyor belt a loop of material that can move objects from one worker or workstation to the next for the steps needed to make a product

countless too many to count

craft (noun) a skill or trade; (verb) to make skillfully, usually by hand

data factual information or details

decade ten-year period

device tool or piece of equipment

devise work out, invent, or plan

domesticate tame

drawback problem or bad side

dwindle become smaller or less

economical inexpensive and efficient

edit cut down to a different or shorter version

fix in photography, to make an image lasting

fuse an electrical safety device

gear a toothed wheel that works as part of a machine

generate create or be the cause of

gesture movement of the body, arms, hands, or legs to express feelings or thoughts

glider a soaring aircraft similar to an airplane but without an engine

harness control, much as an animal may be hitched up and controlled by its harness

hull hard outer shell of a seed or a boat or ship

impaired damaged or limited

imperial having to do with an emperor or empire

implant (noun) object inserted within living tissue; (verb) insert securely or deeply

lens (plural: lenses) curved piece of glass that concentrates rays of light

locomotive railway vehicle that carries the engine that moves train cars along

lunar having to do with the Moon

magnify make something appear larger

manufacture make from raw materials, by hand or by machine

matter physical substance or material from which something is made

method way or system

microphone a device that changes sound to electrical signals, usually in order to record or send sound

mineral naturally occurring nonliving substance

oral having to do with the mouth

paraffin fuel for lanterns

paralyse make someone or something unable to move

patent (verb) legally protect the rights to make, use, or sell an invention; (noun) document that legally protects the ownership and use of an invention

propeller a device that uses blades that fan outwards from a central hub to propel (move) a vehicle, such as a boat or an airplane

pulp mashed-up pasty glop; fleshy material of a soft fruit

radiation energy sent out in the form of rays, waves, or particles

ray beam

recycle to pass used or useless material through various changes in order to create new useful products from it

refinery factory that treats crude petroleum and separates it into different parts

ritual a formal custom or ceremony, often religious

scholarship an award of money to help pay for a person's education

sensitive easily affected

smog dirty air, a word made by combining "**sm**oke" and "**fog**" to describe how the air looks

solar having to do with the Sun

spool reel for winding lengths of materials such as tape, thread, or wire

standard commonly accepted amount or number

storage space to keep or hold on to things

submerge put under water

superior better than

surgery a medical procedure or operation for treating a disease or condition

technology the theories and discoveries of science put into practice in actual actions, machines, and processes

telegraph a device for sending coded messages over long distances by using electrical signals

traditional usual; well known because of custom or longtime use

transmitter a device that sends messages or code

vehicle a device or machine used to carry something

waste materials that are unused or left over after some work or action is finished